Flying Frog Publishing, Inc.
Auburn, Maine 04210 U.S.A.
Copyright © 1996 Flying Frog Publishing, Inc.

NOAH'S ARK

Retold by Ronne Randall
Illustrated by Sara Sliwinska

Flying Frog Publishing

Long, long ago, when the world was still new, there were many wicked people. They did not obey God.

They told lies, they cheated and stole. And they fought and killed one another.

But there was one man who was good. His name was Noah.

Noah was kind and honest and hard-working. In all that he did, he loved God and obeyed him.

One day, God spoke to Noah. He said, "I must put an end to all the wickedness and violence I see. I will send a flood to destroy the world and everyone in it. But I will save you and your family."

God told Noah to build a big ship called an ark. "It must be made of gopher wood, so it will be strong," said God. "And you must cover it with tar, inside and out, so the water cannot get in."

Noah did as God told him. He and his sons, Ham, Shem, and Japheth, worked hard for many days, until the ark was finished.

Then God spoke to Noah again. "Now you must bring in the animals," he said, "every creature that walks or crawls or creeps or hops or flies. Take two of every kind into the ark, one male and one female. And gather in enough food for all the animals, and for your family."

Once more, Noah did as God asked. He brought two of every kind of bird and beast, from the tiniest little ant to the biggest, strongest elephant.

Noah and his wife, and his sons and their wives, stood and watched as the animals boarded the ark.

There were tigers and tortoises, kinkajous and kangaroos, buffalo and bears, porcupines and parrots, antelopes and armadillos, moose and mice and monkeys, and dozens and dozens more. They all came into the ark and settled themselves down.

Then Noah gathered in wheat and corn and barley, and fruits and vegetables — enough food for all the animals, and for himself and his family.

At last the ark was ready. Noah and his family went inside, shut the doors and windows tight, and waited.

Soon the rain began. Thunder boomed and
lightning flashed, and it rained as it had never
rained before. It rained for forty days.

The water rose higher and higher, until all the
earth was flooded. Houses, trees, even mountains,
all were covered by the water that rushed from
the heavens.

But the ark sailed on the waters, strong and safe,
and everyone and everything inside was snug
and dry.

At last the rain stopped. Still the ark sailed on, for another hundred and fifty days, until it came to rest on the top of a mountain called Ararat.

Noah sent a dove out of the ark. But the dove soon came back. So Noah knew it hadn't found any place to land.

A week later, Noah sent the dove out again. It came back with an olive branch in its beak. So Noah knew that the waters had begun to dry up.

Another week passed, and Noah sent the dove out a third time. This time it did not return. It had found a place to land.

Noah opened all the doors and windows of the ark, and he and his family looked out. The waters had dried up, and the world was spread out before them, clean and new again.

Then God spoke to Noah once more, saying, "It is time for you and your family and all the animals to leave the ark and live in the world again. Go forth, and be fruitful and multiply."

When everyone had left the ark, Noah built an altar
and said a prayer of thanks to God.

And God blessed Noah, and said, "I will never
send another flood to destroy the earth — this is
my promise to you. Look up, and I will show you
a special sign."

Noah looked up and saw a most wonderful sight —
a rainbow shining in the heavens.

From that day on, whenever a rainbow has
appeared in the sky, we remember God's promise
to Noah. And we know that God remembers it, too.